ACTS
Book 2 Chapters 13-28

*Amazing
Journeys
With God*

Marilyn Kunz
& Catherine Schell

12 Discussions for Group Bible Study

Neighborhood Bible Studies Publishers

P.O. Box 222

56 Main Street

Dobbs Ferry, NY 10522

1-800-369-0307

e-mail: nbstudies@aol.com

www.NeighborhoodBibleStudy.org

neighborhood bible studies

ISBN 1-880266-04-0
Third Printing January 2005
Printed in the United States of America
Cover photo by Fran Goodrich

GROUP PARTICIPANTS

Name	Address	Phone Number

Copyright ©1993, 1961 by Marilyn Kunz and Catherine Schell

ISBN 1-880266-04-0
Third printing January 2005
Printed in the United States of America
Cover photo by Fran Goodrich

CONTENTS

HOW TO USE THIS DISCUSSION GUIDE

This study guide uses the inductive approach to Bible study. It will help you discover for yourself what the Bible says. It will not give you prepackaged answers. People remember most what they discover for themselves and what they express in their own words. The study guide provides three kinds of questions:

1. What does the passage say? What are the facts?
2. What is the meaning of these facts?
3. How does this passage apply to your life?

Observe the facts carefully before you interpret the meaning of your observations. Then apply the truths you have discovered to life today. Resist the temptation to skip the fact questions since we are not as observant as we think. Find the facts quickly so you can spend more time on their meaning and application.

The purpose of Bible study is not just to know more Bible truths but to apply them. Allow these truths to make a difference in how you think and act, in your attitudes and relationships, in the quality and direction of your life.

Each discussion requires about one hour. Decide on the amount of time to add for socializing and prayer.

Share the leadership. If a different person is the moderator or question-asker each week, interest grows and members feel the group belongs to everyone. The Bible is the authority in the group, not the question-asker.

When a group grows to more than ten, the quiet people become quieter. Plan to grow and multiply. You can meet as two groups in the same house or begin another group so that more people can participate and benefit.

TOOLS FOR AN EFFECTIVE BIBLE STUDY

1. A study guide for each person in the group.
2. A modern translation of the Bible such as:
   NEW INTERNATIONAL VERSION (NIV)
   CONTEMPORARY ENGLISH VERSION (CEV)
   JERUSALEM BIBLE (JB)
   NEW AMERICAN STANDARD BIBLE (NASB)
   REVISED ENGLISH BIBLE (REB)
   NEW REVISED STANDARD VERSION (NRSV)
3. An English dictionary.
4. A map of the Lands of the Bible in a Bible or in the study guide.
5. Your conviction that the Bible is worth studying.

GUIDELINES FOR AN EFFECTIVE STUDY

1. Stick to the passage under discussion.
2. Avoid tangents. If the subject is not addressed in the passage, put it on hold until after the study.
3. Let the Bible speak for itself. Do not quote other authorities or rewrite it to say what you want it to say.
4. Apply the passage personally and honestly.
5. Listen to one another to sharpen your insights.
6. Prepare by reading the Bible passage and thinking through the questions during the week.
7. Begin and end on time.

1. Prepare by reading the passage several times, using different translations if possible. Ask for God's help in understanding it. Consider how the questions might be answered. Observe which questions can be answered quickly and which may require more time.

2. Begin on time.

3. Lead the group in opening prayer or ask someone ahead of time to do so. Don't take anyone by surprise.

4. Ask for a different volunteer to read each Bible section. Read the question. Wait for an answer. Rephrase the question if necessary. Resist the temptation to answer the question yourself. Move to the next question. Skip questions already answered by the discussion.

5. Encourage everyone to participate. Ask the group, "What do the rest of you think?" "What else could be added?"

6. Receive all answers warmly. If needed, ask, "In which verse did you find that?" "How does that fit with verse...?"

7. If a tangent arises, ask, "Do we find the answer to that here?" Or suggest, "Let's write that down and look for the information as we go along."

8. Discourage members who are too talkative by saying, "When I read the next question, let's hear from someone who hasn't spoken yet today."

9. Use the summary questions to bring the study to a conclusion on time.

10. Close the study with prayer.

11. Decide on one person to be the host and another person to ask the questions at the next discussion.

INTRODUCTION

The first twelve chapters of Acts, Luke's account of the thirty years following the resurrection and ascension of Jesus, dealt mainly with events in Jerusalem, Judea and Samaria. The group of 120 believers upon whom the Holy Spirit came at Pentecost grew to many thousands. Persecution triggered by the death of Stephen scattered believers who traveled preaching the gospel message throughout Judea and Samaria and up the Mediterranean coast to Antioch in Syria. In the process, Samaritans and Gentiles were baptized in the name of Jesus Christ and received the gift of the Holy Spirit. At this point, the writer of the book of Acts turns the focus of his account from Jerusalem and the ministry of the twelve apostles to Syrian Antioch and the missionary journeys of Saul and Barnabas.

DISCUSSION 1

First Missionary Journey Begins

ACTS 13

Since Barnabas originally came from Cyprus (4:36) and he and Saul have spent a year in Syrian Antioch teaching the new church (11:25, 26), it is logical that they begin their first outreach journey at Antioch and move on to Cyprus. John Mark from Jerusalem (12:25) accompanies them.

READ ACTS 13:1-12

1. How and why do Barnabas and Saul leave the church at Antioch?

2. Describe the situation Barnabas and Saul encounter at Paphos.

3. What does Saul accuse Elymas of doing?

   How is the matter settled and with what result?

*Note: Notice that from this point in the narrative, Saul is called by his Greek name, Paul. Paul's increasing leadership is indicated (verse 9) by Luke's references hereafter to **Paul and Barnabas**, or **Paul and his companions**.*

READ ACTS 13:13-43

4. Trace the journey from Syrian Antioch to Seleucia, Salamis and Paphos in Cyprus, to Antioch of Pisidia on the map on pages 36-37.

   What opportunity does Paul use (verses 5, 14, 15)?

5. Analyze Paul's first recorded sermon (verses 16-41) by answering the following questions:

   a. What are the specific acts of God which Paul mentions from:

      –the ancient history of Israel (verses 17-22)?

      –the recent history of Israel (verses 23, 30, 37)?

   b. What connection and what distinction does Paul make between David and Jesus (verses 22, 23, 32-37)?

   c. What was the ministry and testimony of John the Baptist (verses 24, 25)?

d. What did the people in Jerusalem and their leaders do with the promised Savior that God sent (verses 27-29)?

e. What does Paul see to be his own function in the plan of God (verses 26, 32, 38)?

f. What opportunity and warning does he present to his hearers (verses 38-40)?

6. How do Paul's listeners in the synagogue respond?

READ ACTS 13:44-52

7. When most of the city gathers on the next sabbath to hear the word of the Lord, many Jews and devout converts to Judaism follow Paul and Barnabas, but some of the Jews jealously speak against what Paul says. How do Paul and Barnabas handle this opposition?

8. What terrible conclusion must be drawn concerning one who rejects the word of God?

9. How do the Gentiles respond to Paul's announcement?

10. How do the unbelieving Jews manage to get rid of Paul and Barnabas?

How do you account for the missionaries' reaction to being expelled?

SUMMARY

1. What characteristics of the church at Antioch would you like to see in your church (verses 1–3)?

2. Paul and Barnabas have already traveled over 400 miles since they were commissioned to carry the gospel from the church at Antioch in Syria. How would you evaluate the success of this mission to Antioch of Pisidia?

3. How does God's standard for success differ from ours?

PRAYER

O God, thank you that forgiveness of sins is open to us through your Son, the Lord Jesus Christ, and that this salvation is available to Jews and to Gentiles. May our lives be filled with your joy and your Holy Spirit. Amen.

DISCUSSION 2

First Missionary Journey Completed

ACTS 14

Although persecution against Paul and Barnabas has forced their departure from Pisidian Antioch, they leave behind them a thriving group of Christians from both Jewish and Gentile backgrounds. The missionaries now move on about ninety miles to Iconium, a prosperous commercial city on one of the major trade routes and the home of many Jews.

READ ACTS 14:1-23

1. Why, do you think, do Paul and Barnabas always go first to the synagogue to preach?
   largest audience in the place

   What sort of reception do they get in this synagogue?
   A great number become believers, but the unbelieving Jews tried to turn people against them

2. What two factors are at work in verses 1-4 and with what result?
   Apostles v. Jews
   The city becomes divided.

3. Consider the opposing forces at work in your own life, one to poison your mind against the gospel, the other to bear witness to the word of the Lord.

Are you divided in your response to the gospel? Why or why not?

4. What situation causes Paul and Barnabas to leave Iconium? *Fear of being stoned.*

   Locate Lystra and Derbe in relation to Iconium on your map. Notice that these missionaries flee forward they do not retreat.

5. When Paul encounters the crippled man in Lystra, why does he consider healing him? *The man had the faith to be healed.*

6. When this man who has never walked jumps up and begins to walk, how does the crowd react? *Thought Paul & Barnabus were gods.*

   What do you learn about the religion of the people of Lystra? *Belief in greek gods.*

7. Compare the reception of Paul and Barnabas here, even from the priest of Zeus, with their reception among the Jews, particularly the religious rulers of the Jews, in Iconium. *The Jews wanted to stone them. and crowds in Lystra praised them.*

Note: There was an ancient legend in Lystra that the gods Zeus and Hermes had once visited that land but only one old peasant couple had given them hospitality. In consequence, everyone else was destroyed by the gods. Paul's healing miracle causes the people to feel the gods have visited them again.

8. How do Paul and Barnabas react to the people's intention?

We are just mortals, bringing you the good news

Since the people of Lystra have no Jewish background, where do Paul and Barnabas start in their preaching and what do they teach about the living God?

Created heaven + earth meeting every need

9. What happens to hinder their ministry in Lystra?

Jews came a won over crowds, stoned him a left him for dead

How serious are Paul's injuries?

He got up + left city

10. What impresses you about the courage and tenacity of Paul and Barnabas in verses 21-23, in light of what has recently happened to them in Lystra, Iconium and Antioch?

They continue to bravely spread the good news

11. What five things do Paul and Barnabas do as they revisit the new Christians before returning home?

strengthened souls of disciples, encouraged them in their faith. appointed elders in each church, prayer a fasting entrusted to Lord

How are these things vital to the survival and growth of these young churches?

strengthens by example

READ ACTS 14:24–28

12. Trace on the map the return trip to Antioch. What report do the missionaries bring back to the church which sent them out?

related all they had done & how God opened door of faith

What do they emphasize rather than their discomfort and persecutions?

positive experience - work completed thru grace of God.

SUMMARY

1. Acts 13 and 14 recount the events of Paul's first missionary journey. From these two chapters, what is Paul's message?

   What are his methods?

2. Consider your own responsibility as a Christian to proclaim the gospel, to strengthen disciples and to exhort Christian friends to continue in the faith. How can you do this by letter, phone call, or visit this week?

3. What traits of character exhibited by Paul and Barnabas in this chapter do you want to develop in your life?

PRAYER

O Lord, we are amazed at the zeal and courage of your servants in the events of these chapters. Thank you for their example. Strengthen us, we pray, to speak your word today wherever you send us. Grant that we may be true to the faith Paul and Barnabas proclaimed which has come to us because many others have been faithful.

DISCUSSION *3*

Council at Jerusalem

ACTS 15:1-35

Sent out by the church at Antioch in Syria, Paul and Barnabas proclaim the good news of Christ on the island of Cyprus, and then in the regions of Pamphylia and Pisidia. The two missionaries establish churches to whom Paul later writes his letter to the Galatians. They concentrate their ministry at the important points along the main highways between Jerusalem and Rome. In each place, they take the message of forgiveness of sins through Christ to the local synagogue first. Large numbers of Gentiles respond to Paul's message of equal rights with Jewish believers before God without the need to observe ceremonial law.

READ ACTS 15:1-5

1. Jewish and Gentile believers came to Antioch telling the good news about Jesus. As both groups believed, the interracial church developed with gifted teachers and prophets. What problem do visitors introduce in the church in Antioch (verses 1, 2)?

   Necessary to be circumcised - keep law of Moses

   What do the Christians there decide to do?

Note: The question at issue is whether a Gentile has to become a Jew by circumcision and obedience to the Law of Moses before he can become a Christian. And even if Gentiles are allowed into the church, to what extent can they mingle *with Jewish believers in the social life of the church? Remember God's lesson to Peter to prepare him to visit Cornelius...**"Do not call anything impure"** (Acts 10:15).*

2. Compare the reaction of the Phoenician and Samaritan believers with the reaction of the believers among the Pharisees (verses 3-5) when they receive the news of the conversion of the Gentiles.

   Believers found great joy in conversions
   Pharisees focused on law & obedience

   What do some of the Jewish Christians consider necessary for salvation?

READ ACTS 15:6-21

3. As the apostles and elders meet in this first church council at Jerusalem, what position does Peter take on the matter under debate?

   God cleansed our hearts by faith
   & made no distinction among us

   What reasons does he state?

   gave us the Holy Spirit

4. According to Peter, what is the basis for salvation for both Jew and Gentile?

   We are saved thru the grace of Jesus

5. What do Paul and Barnabas contribute to the conference?

   Told of signs & wonders

   Describe in a few sentences their experiences in chapters 13 and 14 which are referred to in verse 12.

   Healing of crippled man
   Blinding of Elymas

6. James, the brother of the Lord and a careful observer of the law, seems to be officiating at the conference. What points does he make in his argument?

God looks favorably on Gentiles - taking a people for his name. Not trouble

*Note: In verse 14 James refers to Peter by his Jewish name, **Simon** or **Symeon** (RSV).*

7. What judgment does James make in conclusion (verses 19-21)?

Not trouble newly converted, but ask them to abstain from certain things.

How does he use the Old Testament scripture to test the validity of their experience?

So all peoples may seek the Lord.

8. What place do past experience and the word of God have in your decisions?

Why is it necessary that these two agree?

READ ACTS 15:22-35

Note: The council accepted the decision stated by James that the Gentiles should avoid sexual impurity, foods offered to idols, and meat not killed in the Jewish way (in which the blood was drained off). If Gentile believers would keep these simple rules, there would be no barrier to fellowship and social contact between Jews and Gentiles within the Christian church.

9. How does the conference implement its decision?
Send men to Antioch w/ Paul + Barnabas

What would be the value of sending both an official letter and representatives from the Jewish church to explain the decisions in person?
authority of the church

10. Describe the tone of the letter and its contents.
Reassuring- sets requirements clearly .

11. Judas and Silas, leaders among the Christians at Jerusalem, present the Jerusalem position and decision. How does the church at Antioch accept the letter?
They rejoiced at contents .

12. Why is this decision of the council so important to the church at Antioch?
Encourages + strengthens the church .

What sort of things do you think Judas and Silas said to strengthen the Christians at Antioch?
Good news of Jesus Christ

SUMMARY

1. In this chapter what major crisis arises in the church?
Division of church

2. What effect has the Jerusalem council's decision had upon the church down to the present time?
Dietary rules + sexual prohibitions

3. Today there are still some who insist there is something a person must do, some work he or she must perform, in order to be saved. Some others fail to teach the necessity of salvation. What does Acts 15 teach about salvation and who is saved?

   We are saved by grace of Jesus Christ.

PRAYER

O God, we praise you for providing your salvation to Jews and Gentiles through the grace of the Lord Jesus. Thank you that you purify our hearts by faith, not by keeping the Law you gave your people before the coming of the Messiah. Grant that men and women today, Jews and Gentiles, may seek you and come to bear your name. For Jesus' sake, we pray. Amen.

DISCUSSION

4

Second Missionary Journey - Philippi

ACTS 15:36—16:40

When the number of Gentile believers multiplied on the first missionary journey of Paul and Barnabas, conditions arose which could have split the young church into two bodies, one Jewish and one Gentile. After thorough discussion of the whole matter, the Council of Jerusalem stated clearly that salvation for both Jew and Gentile was by faith alone in Jesus Christ. With Gentile Christians asked to respect Jewish scruples about food, and to abstain from sexual immorality, there was nothing to hinder social fellowship within the church.

READ ACTS 15:36-41

1. When Paul and Barnabas decide to make a return visit to the Christian groups formed on their first journey, what is the basis of the disagreement between them? Barnabas wanted to take Mark Paul did not b/c he had deserted them.

    How does each reveal his personality in the position he takes? Barnabas took Mark & sailed to Cyprus Paul took Silas, going through Syria & Cicilia.

2. What do you know about Paul's new companion (15: 22, 32)? prophet & leader among brothers

READ ACTS 16:1-5

3. Trace on the map the beginning of this second missionary journey: Antioch, Syria, Cilicia, Derbe, Lystra.

4. Why does Paul return to Lystra where he was almost stoned to death (14:8-20)?

   to see how they were doing

5. Describe Timothy's background and character.

   son of a Jewish woman - believer. + Greek father. Well spoken of by believers in Lystra + Iconium

   What special circumstances in Timothy's background cause Paul to circumcise Timothy (verses 1, 3)?

   Father was Greek

Note: To Jewish eyes, Timothy as the uncircumcised child of a mixed marriage would be considered illegitimate.

6. What effect do the visit of Paul and Silas and their news have upon the churches?

   strengthened in faith increased in numbers daily

7. Think about people you know in whose presence you are strengthened in the Christian faith. What qualities in these people produce this effect on your life?

   great faith   comfortable familiarity strong prayer life   with Scripture

READ ACTS 16:6-15

Note: This incident in which the gospel crosses the sea from Asia Minor to Europe has affected the whole of world history since. Macedonia was the northern section of what we call Greece *today. Trace on the map the journey from Lystra to Troas to Philippi. The use of the pronoun **we** (verses 10, 11) <u>indicates Luke's presence with the company from this point.</u>*

8. In what various ways do Paul and his company experience God's guidance in verses 6-10?

Forbidden to speak word in Asia
Forbidden to enter Bithynia
Urged to cross over to Macedonia.

9. Paul is guided because he is committed beforehand to absolute obedience to God. Compare yourself with Paul on the following:

   -a basic desire to communicate the gospel.

   -sensitivity to the Holy Spirit.

   -willingness to obey the guidance of God.

10. Though Philippi is a Roman colony and the leading city of that district, apparently it has no synagogue. On the Sabbath, how does Paul find worshipers of God? *Outside gate by river - a place of prayer*

11. Describe Lydia, the first convert to Christ in Europe.
Worshipper of god from Thyatira, dealer in purple cloth

   From what you see in Lydia, what attitudes and actions should alert you to modern day women and men who are seeking to know God? *God opens our hearts to believe His word*

12. How does Paul handle the uncomfortable situation that arises with the slave girl?

orders the spirit to come out of her in the name of Jesus.

13. What are the consequences for Paul and Silas of the slave girl's release?

seized P + S + brought in front of magistrates - flogged + jailed

14. Instead of moaning and complaining at their exceedingly unjust and uncomfortable situation, Paul and Silas are praying and singing at midnight. What effect do they have on all the prisoners and the jailer?

15. Describe the jailer's emotions, fears, questions, and responses. *He was about to kill himself b/c prisoners escape.*

What happens between his fear (verse 29) and his joy (verse 34)? *He believed, heard the word of god, ministered to them + was baptized.*

In what sense has the jailer been the true captive? *Captive in his role of jailer + obedience to authorities*

READ ACTS 16:35-40

16. How would an apology from the magistrates affect the status of the church which Paul is leaving behind in Philippi?

Why is it important for Paul and Silas to meet with the Christians before they leave Philippi? *to encourage + strengthen the believers*

SUMMARY

1. Compare Lydia, the slave girl, and the jailer as to their background, need, and the work of God in each life.

   How have you seen God intervene in the lives of people like each of them?

2. Lydia, a woman with money, position, and respectability, even a worshiper of God, <u>still needed God to open her heart that she might receive the Lord Jesus Christ as her Savior</u>. What has God used to open your heart in this way to receive Jesus Christ?

3. During this coming week, read the letter Paul wrote some years later to this group of Christians, the letter of Paul to the Philippians. As you read it, keep in mind the people and the circumstances involved in the founding of this church.

PRAYER

O God, thank you for sending Paul and Silas to Europe with the news that your salvation is available to all through Jesus Christ. We praise you for their faithfulness in sharing that good news with men and women of all backgrounds, wherever you sent them. Give us sensitivity and courage to follow their example. For Jesus' sake, Amen.

DISCUSSION 5

Thessalonica, Berea, Athens

ACTS 17

, one of elders from Jerusalem

Paul, accompanied by Silas from the church in Jerusalem, has been visiting the churches begun on his first missionary journey, to see how they are and to deliver the decisions reached at the recent Council of Jerusalem. Directed by the Holy Spirit from Asia to Europe, Paul and his companions meet Lydia, a business woman in Philippi and a worshiper of God. In response to Paul's message, the first church in Europe is established in her household. Later when Paul and Silas are beaten and jailed, their imprisonment and release lead to the conversion of the jailer and his household. Escorted out of Philippi, the missionaries travel on a hundred miles to Thessalonica.

READ ACTS 17:1-9

1. How does Paul's ministry at Thessalonica differ from that at Philippi?

   Synagogue of the jews at Philippi

   What two points does he emphasize in his preaching at Thessalonica (verse 3)?

   god fearer - followed Jewish customs - converted - became proselytes.

   Necessary for Jesus to suffer + rise from the dead. that he was the Messiah contrary to what Jews believed

2. Who responds positively to this ministry?

   great many of devout Greeks + leading women some Jews

   Where do the jealous Jews get their allies?

   ruffians in market place formed a mob center of town

3. Compare the opposition from the Jews here with that from the Gentiles at Philippi.

dragged Jason + believers to magistrates instead of Paul + Silas

What is the cause in each place?

fear / jealousy

Gentiles listened
Jews had evil intent

4. Whom do these Jews prefer to Jesus (verse 7)?

the Emperor Caesar

What allegiances may people choose today when they reject Jesus as Lord?

wealth, career, other religions consumerism

READ ACTS 17:10-15

5. What part do the Old Testament scriptures play in Paul's ministry to the Jews at Berea?

Examined the scriptures daily - looked at scriptures welcoming message to see if what Paul said was true

What are the results and why?

more receptive + becoming believers many Jews believed.

6. The Bereans believed Paul's message after they found it consistent with the Old Testament Scriptures. They moved from examining the Scriptures to belief in Jesus Christ. How has the study of the Bible affected your life?

Paul went to synagogue - people who should understand the message + respond.

7. News that Paul is preaching in Berea brings certain Jews sixty miles from the big city of Thessalonica to the small town of Berea. What indicates that Paul has become the main object of opposition (verse 14)?

sent Paul away to the coast for his own protection

READ ACTS 17:16-34

8. While waiting for Silas and Timothy to join him from Berea, where and how does Paul spend his time in Athens?

preaching / arguing in synagogue + marketplace reasoning

9. What message does Paul carry to the market place?

the good news of Jesus

10. Stoic philosophers believed self-sufficiency was the highest good, while the Epicureans pursued pleasure. How do they react to what Paul is saying (verses 18-21)?

good news about Jesus + resurrection

Note: In Paul's time, one of the functions of the Court of Areopagus, the most ancient institution of Athens, was to examine and license public lectures.

11. Why does Paul begin his message at Athens differently from his preaching in other places?

Acknowleges their religious nature presents a very logical explanation to logical people

O.T. would not have made any impact on these people

Why does he emphasize these particular facts about God before he presents Christ to them?

Because they are searching for God - who is not far from us.
center altar is altar to "unknown God."

12. When Paul calls upon the Athenians with all people everywhere to repent, what reasons does he give for them to take his call seriously?

God has overlooked our ignorance but now he has fixed a day to judge the world by Jesus Christ. everyone will be accountable.

13. At what point in this sermon do Paul's hearers begin to react?

• Some scoffed at the resurrection - • some wanted to hear more ..some believed.

Which of the three responses from the hearers would you expect to such a sermon today?

Wanting to hear more - believing.

SUMMARY

1. Today radio and television talk shows provide the opportunity for *doing nothing but talking about and listening to the latest ideas.* How can you avoid the danger of fitting into the Athenian type (verses 21)?

culture + locality affect churches secularism keep your eye on + selective about what you listen to - outreach

2. Thessalonica was a thriving trade center, Berea a smaller town inland to the west, and Athens the great intellectual and cultural center of the world in Paul's time. How do you account for the various reactions to the gospel in these three cities?

money the material world - jealous

As a result - different # of believers

willing to discuss + debate -

Bible study

willing to listen, examine scriptures

3. During the week, read the <u>letters of 1 and 2 Thessalonians,</u> written later by Paul to the church at Thessalonica. Remember the people and events that started the church.

summer homework

PRAYER

Lord God, we acknowledge you as the creator of the world and everything in it. We worship you as the Lord of heaven and earth who gives us life and breath and everything we possess, so that we live and move and have our being in you. Most of all we would love and serve you because you have sent your Son Jesus Christ to be our Savior. We pray and praise you in his name. Amen.

Sept 8th

DISCUSSION

6

Third Missionary Journey Begins

ACTS 18

Paul has been forced to move on from Thessalonica and then from Berea by the agitation of some Jews jealous at the large number of Jews and Gentiles who believe Paul's message. While waiting in Athens for Silas and Timothy to join him, Paul has preached the gospel in the market place and in the meeting of the Aeropagus to philosophers and skeptics. A few have believed and joined him.

READ ACTS 18:1-11

1. Unlike his departure from Thessalonica and Berea, Paul apparently leaves Athens of his own accord. Find his next step, *Corinth*, on your map. The key city of Achaia, Corinth was the crossroads of commercial traffic in Greece, the home of the Isthmian games that were second only to the Olympics, and the location of a temple of Aphrodite with its multitude of priestess-prostitutes.

   a city of sin - sexual relationships.

2. What factors bring Paul, Aquila and Priscilla together in Corinth?

   They were both tentmakers,
   P & A thrown out of Rome by Claudius.

   What do you think they discuss as they work? *their faith*

   The Good News -
   Jesus is the Messiah.

3. How and why do Paul's activities change when Silas and Timothy arrive?

He devoted himself exclusively to preaching.

4. What problems and what encouragements does Paul have in this city?

Opposition from the Jews. support from the synagogue rulers + other believers

How do you account for his prolonged stay here?

The Lord spoke to him in a vision, telling Paul he would be safe from harm.

5. What has God used to encourage you when problems overwhelmed you?

Angels of mercy to help and support.

READ ACTS 18:12-23

6. What accusation is made against Paul?

He was accused of persuading people to worship God in a religion not recognized by Roman law.

By whom, and to whom is it made?

Accused by the Jews & brought to court before Gallio, the proconsul.

7. How does Gallio, the Roman proconsul, handle the proceedings? *He said the accusation involved words and names & not serious crimes - so he told them to settle it themselv*

How is the Lord fulfilling the promise he made months before to Paul (verses 9, 10)?

I am with you and no one is going to attack and harm you.

8. When Paul leaves Corinth for Syria, Priscilla and Aquila accompany him as far as Ephesus. How do the Jews there respond to Paul's message?

They asked him to spend more time with them.

Why would it be important for Priscilla and Aquila to *Encounter w/ Apollos*
remain here when Paul leaves?

They would give valuable aid upon P's return - providing advice as to where + how work could be started.

9. Trace on the map Paul's journey from Corinth to Antioch (verses 18-22) and the beginning of his third missionary journey (verse 23).

10. *He went up and greeted the church* (verse 22) apparently refers to the church at Jerusalem. Why would Paul visit both the Jerusalem and Antioch churches at the conclusion of this second missionary journey?

To have as much exposure + to gain as many believers as possible. The apostles are in Jerusalem. Antioch is the center of the church.

READ ACTS 18:24-28

11. Locate Alexandria, Ephesus, and Achaia on your map.

12. What might a reporter in Ephesus write about Apollos, after hearing this visiting lecturer from Alexandria? *He was a learned man. With knowledge of scripture. He knew about Jesus but still looking forward to coming of Messiah.*

13. How do you account for Priscilla and Aquila's invitation and instruction to the learned Apollos? *To give him the accurate story of Jesus Christ.*

14. How is Apollos' preaching and ministry in Achaia enhanced by his stop in Ephesus? *He vigorously refuted the Jews in public debate, proving from scripture that Jesus was the Christ.*

baptism of repentance vs. baptism of salvation

SUMMARY

1. Consider the Christians in this chapter:

   –Paul.

   –Priscilla and Aquila. - A

   –Silas and Timothy.

   –Crispus.

   –many Corinthians who believed.

   –Apollos. - A Jew

   How are they alike and how are they different?
   All believers who were Jews
   of different social status - background

   Why do they need each other?
   To teach, to support and encourage each
   other, to enable the Good News to be
   spread further over a wider geographical
   area.

2. How have individuals and groups helped you in
   your Christian faith and obedience?
   Cursillo   Spiritual   to more
   Prayer chains   Direction   people

   To whom can you be an encourager?
   Sponsoring cursillo candidates   Sonshine
   Grouping   Ministry
   w/treya   Prayer Shawl
                                       Ministry

3. During the coming week, read quickly through
   Paul's two letters, 1 and 2 Corinthians, written later
   to the church at Corinth. As you read, keep in
   mind the events surrounding the founding of the
   church there.

PRAYER

Thank you, Lord, for the ways you blessed and used men and women of such different backgrounds to spread the gospel message in the world of Paul's day. Thank you for the power of your work to change lives, and to build your church. Use us, we pray, as your servants in our time and in our world. For Jesus' sake, Amen.

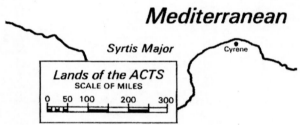

Mediterranean

Syrtis Major

Cyrene

Lands of the ACTS
SCALE OF MILES

0   50 100   200   300

8-22-08

7

Ephesus

ACTS 19

Paul's ministry for eighteen month at Corinth produces a growing church thee. Leaving Priscilla and Aquila at Ephesus, Paul completes his second missionary journey, spending some time at his home church in Antioch. Paul begins a third journey strengthening the Christians throughout Galatia and Phrygia. Meanwhile, Apollos, a learned Jewish scholar who teaches about Jesus, comes to Ephesus where Priscilla and Aquila instruct him further in the Christian faith. After Apollos departs for Corinth, Paul arrives in Ephesus.

READ ACTS 19:1-20

1. What does Paul learn about these disciples at Ephesus from the two questions he asks them?

What change comes to their lives through Paul's ministry?

2. Describe Paul's preaching at Ephesus and the opposition to it.

What is the result of this opposition (verses 8-10)?

3. Why do stubbornness, disbelief, and speaking against the gospel frequently occur in that order in people who do not receive Jesus as Lord although the truth is clearly presented to them?

4. How is Paul's previous experience at Corinth (18:5-7) being repeated at Ephesus (19:8, 9)?

5. Why would Paul stay longer in the strategic locations of Corinth in Greece and Ephesus in Asia Minor (18:11,18; 19:10)?

6. In what different ways does God manifest his power at Ephesus (verses 11-16)?

7. What does the attempt of the sons of Sceva to use the name of Jesus teach the people of Ephesus, the believers, and those who practice magic?

8. What costly action do many people take?

With what results (verses 18-20)?

What forms of sorcery or magic might Christians need to get rid of today?

9. Why is it not enough merely to pronounce the name of the Lord Jesus in order to be a Christian or to be a recipient of his power?

READ ACTS 19:21-41

10. What does Paul plan to do when he leaves Ephesus?

11. Exactly what provokes the next opposition to Paul's ministry (verses 23-27)?

How does this opposition differ from that described in verses 8, 9?

12. From Demetrius' speech to the silversmith's guild, what do you learn about the changes the gospel is making in that whole region?

13. Why is Demetrius able to arouse such a violent response from his hearers?

Describe the reactions of the crowd in the near-riot that follows (verses 28-40).

Give an example of situations today in which people in crowds react in these same ways.

14. What arguments does the town clerk use to disperse the crowd?

Why is he able to handle them successfully when Alexander could not?

SUMMARY

1. Paul's stay in Ephesus is the major part of his third missionary journey. How do you evaluate the positive and negative effects his visit has on this area?

2. During this week, read Paul's letter to the Ephesians, written several years later, probably while he is a prisoner at Rome. As you read Ephesians, keep in mind the tumultuous events associated with Paul's ministry here during the Ephesian church's early years.

PRAYER

Lord Jesus, we thank you for the power of your name to deliver from evil and to transform the lives of those who put their trust in you. May we be as willing to put away any evil in our lives as the Ephesians were who burned their scrolls and recognized that gods made by human beings are no gods at all. Deliver us from trusting in anything or anyone beside you. Amen.

DISCUSSION

Paul's Farewells - Third Journey Ends

ACTS 20 21:16

During Paul's two and a half years' ministry in Ephesus the word of the Lord spreads through the province of Asia. So many believe in the gospel and stop buying shrines of Artemis that craftsmen blame Paul's preaching for their loss of business. Demetrius instigates a near-riot against him. When the city clerk dismisses the assembly, he refers the craftsmen to the courts if they wish to press charges against Paul.

READ ACTS 20:1-12

1. Trace on your map Paul's journey from Ephesus through Macedonia to Greece and back to Troas.

    Why does Paul change his plans?

2. Considering some of the conditions and pressures under which these early Christians lived, what do you think Paul emphasizes as he exhorts and encourages them (verses 1, 2)?

    What sort of exhortation and encouragement do you need as a Christian today?

3. On Sunday the church in Troas meets to break bread, the Lord's supper, a characteristic of the young church from its beginning in Jerusalem (2:42). Why does Paul preach so long?

Why are they willing to listen for so long?

4. What effect would Euthychus' accident have on this young church?

READ ACTS 20:13-38

5. Continue to trace Paul's journey.

Why would being in Jerusalem for the feast of Pentecost be especially significant to Paul and his fellow Christians?

6. To save Paul time, the elders of the church at Ephesus come to Miletus to see him. In his farewell address to them Paul describes his past ministry at Ephesus. What are (is):

-his attitudes and aims (verses 19, 20, 26, 27, 33-35)?

-his message (verses 21, 24, 25, 27)?

-his methods (verses 20, 21, 25, 31, 34, 35)?

-the difficulties he faced (verse 19)?

7. From Paul's statement of his supreme aim in life (verse 24) what matters to him and what does not matter?

   How would you state your aim in life?

8. What dangers does he predict in the future for the church at Ephesus (verses 28-30)?

   What strong advice does he give for dealing with these dangers (verses 28, 31, 32)?

9. In whose care does Paul leave the Ephesian church and elders (verse 32)?

10. How do you balance the need to be on guard against distorters of the truth and trusting confidently in God's word?

READ ACTS 21:1-16

11. Continue to trace on your map Paul's journey to Jerusalem.

12. What do the farewells at Tyre and Miletus (20:36-38) reveal about the personal relationship between Paul and his fellow disciples?

13. How would Agabus' graphic warning have affected you if you had been one of Paul's companions?

14. Why doesn't Paul heed those who don't want him to go to Jerusalem? See 20:22-24; 19:21.

   How can you determine when you are following God's priorities?

15. How do his friends accept his refusal (verse 14)?

SUMMARY

1. As Paul arrives in Jerusalem he concludes his third and last recorded missionary journey. Compare Paul's three journeys by completing the following chart:

	First	Second	Third
Territory covered			
Message preached			
Methods used			
Responses			

2. What do you learn about God's purposes, power, and grace from the events of these missionary journeys?

PRAYER

O Lord, we thank you for the perseverance of your servant Paul and his companions in proclaiming the gospel and teaching the young churches throughout the Mediterranean world. Help us to serve you as faithfully today in our world. For your name's sake, Amen.

DISCUSSION 9

Paul's Arrest at Jerusalem

ACTS 21:17—22:30

In spite of the prophet Agabus' warning and the pleas of Paul's friends, Paul comes to Jerusalem, intending to go on to Rome and then to Spain.

READ ACTS 21:17-26

1. In Jerusalem, James and the church elders praise God for Paul's report of what God has done among the Gentiles. But they foresee a problem among the Jewish believers. What problem or danger has arisen from a false report about Paul?

2. What specific action on Paul's part do the elders think would solve the problem?

    To what extent is Paul willing to go for the sake of the unity of the church?

Note: Years later Paul explained: Though I am free and belong to no man, I make myself a slave to everyone, to win as many as possible. To the Jews I became like a Jew, to win the Jews. To those under the law I became like one under the law (though I myself am not under the law), so as to win those under the law. 1 Corinthians 9:19, 20.

3. What limits might you put on your freedom for the sake of unity in your church, your family, or among your Christian friends?

4. How is the issue raised here (verse 21) different from the one at the Jerusalem council in Acts 15:1, 3-5?

READ ACTS 21:27-40

5. Describe the events leading up to Paul's arrest.

   What mistaken assumption and accusation does the group opposing Paul make?

6. Describe Paul's rescue.

   Why is he permitted to address the crowd?

7. Paul uses every opportunity to advance the gospel. What opportunities do you have to tell what God has done in your life?

READ ACTS 22:1-21

8. Because Paul speaks to the crowd in Aramaic, their native language, the crowd is willing to listen to his defense. If you were a reporter at the scene, how would you describe what you see and hear?

9. How should Paul's description of himself, his background, and his past associations with the high priest and Jewish council affect the attitude of the crowd toward him?

10. Paul devotes the major part of his defense to his experience on the road to Damascus and his meeting with Ananias (verses 6-16). What change in Paul's thinking did this event produce?

11. What effect should Paul's description of Ananias and his message have on those now listening to Paul (verses 12, 14)?

12. What commission does Ananias say the God of our fathers is giving to Paul?

13. Why does Paul think his encounter with God in the temple should persuade his fellow Jews to accept his testimony (verses 17-21) ?

14. At the word Gentile the crowd explodes. Why do they react so violently to the idea of God's concern for the Gentiles, rather than to Paul's clear statement that Jesus of Nazareth is the Messiah?

15. From the tribune's actions, what insight do you get into Roman procedures (verses 23-29)?

16. Now that Paul cannot be tortured into a confession, how does the tribune determine to discover the truth (verse 30)?

SUMMARY

1. What is the main point of Paul's defense?

   Why is his argument irrefutable?

2. What element in Paul's defense is necessary for every Christian's testimony?

3. Ask one or two people in the group to share briefly how they came to recognize Jesus Christ as their Savior and Lord.

PRAYER

O Lord, when we think about the opposition and the dangers Paul experienced as he proclaimed the gospel and sought to unite Jews and Gentiles in Christ, the troubles and pressures of our lives seem small be comparison. Thank you for protecting and strengthening your servants. Help us to be as steadfast as Paul was in serving you. For your name's sake we pray. Amen.

DISCUSSION *10*

Plot Against Paul - Defense Before Felix

ACTS 23 —24

While Paul was in Jerusalem fulfilling a vow in the temple, Jews from Asia stirred up a crowd against him. But the commander of the Roman garrison broke up the resulting riot and rescued Paul. Determined to find out the cause of the disturbance, he ordered the chief priests and Sanhedrin to assemble and now brings Paul before them.

READ ACTS 23:1-10

1. Why does the high priest react so strongly to Paul's declaration of a good conscience before God?

   Why does Paul respond to the blow as he does (verses 3-5)?

2. How does Paul effectively divide the council (verses 6-9)?

   At what point does the commander again have to rescue Paul?

3. Remembering what Paul has been through since his return to Jerusalem, why would he especially need the assurance God gives at this point (verse 11)?

4. What plot develops and who becomes involved in this conspiracy to murder?

   How committed are these conspirators?

5. What means does God use to deliver his servant from this plot?

READ ACTS 23:23-35

6. In this period of Felix's rule, fanatical armed bands of Jewish Zealots stirring up rebellion against Rome prowled the hilly countryside. With the plot against Paul, this company of travelers is in danger of ambush until they reach the open flat country at Antipatris. In light of this, what precautions does the commander take?

Note: The tribune's provision of mounts (plural) for Paul to ride implies Paul's friends are with him.

7. How does Claudius Lysias describe the circumstances of Paul's arrest in such a way as to put himself in a good light with the governor?

How does he describe the charges against Paul?

8. Why does the governor postpone Paul's hearing?

9. Today who demonstrates the zeal, earnestness and courage to the extent Paul does in this chapter?

   What steps can you take individually and as a group toward more commitment and courage in witnessing for Christ?

READ ACTS 24:1-21

Note: The high priest demonstrates the strength of his interest in Paul's case by coming with the Jewish elders from Jerusalem to the Roman headquarters at Caesarea.

10. How does Tertullus word his charges against Paul in such a way that a Roman governor must pay attention to them?

    What loaded words does he use?

11. This is the third time in less than two weeks that Paul has had to speak in the defense of his life. Contrast Paul's opening remarks to Felix with those of Tertullus. How does Paul answer each of the four charges made against him?

12. What does Paul believe about the Scriptures, about the future, and about personal character (verses 14–16)?

    If you agree with Paul on these issues, what effect does this have upon your life?

READ ACTS 24:22-27

13. What impressions do you get of Felix?

    Why doesn't he acquit Paul?

14. Later in a private interview Paul talks with Felix and his Jewish wife about faith in Jesus the Messiah. What elements in Paul's preaching alarm Felix? Why?

SUMMARY

1. The difficult circumstances in Acts 23 and 24 may be the very situations in which Paul learned the secret of Christ's inner strengthening. What are you learning in the circumstances you face?

2. Although the Roman governor Felix had many opportunities to believe the gospel, he typifies the person whose exposure to the gospel ends in tragedy. What forces within Felix contribute to this result?

How are you, or people you know, in similar danger? Why?

PRAYER

O Lord, we praise you for protecting and strengthening your servant Paul. Help us to trust you as he did. We are glad that this world and its imperfect justice is not all there is. Thank you that we have the same hope Paul had, that the day is coming when there will be a resurrection of the just and the unjust, when you will right wrongs and give perfect justice. Amen.

DISCUSSION

11

Paul's Defense Before Festus and Agrippa

ACTS 25—26

Two years have passed since Paul's arrest in the temple in Jerusalem and his imprisonment in Herod's palace in Caesarea. Hoping for a bribe from Paul and seeking to placate the Jews, the Roman governor Felix continually postpones making a decision in Paul's case. Though kept under guard, Paul is allowed some freedom and his friends are permitted to take care of his needs.

Felix, called back to Rome because he failed to deal effectively with riots between Jews and Gentiles in Caesarea, leaves Paul's case for the new governor Festus to decide. The Jewish leaders show their continuing hatred of Paul by promptly appearing before Festus to press their charges against Paul.

READ ACTS 25:1-12

1. Festus refuses the Jewish leaders' request to move Paul's trial to Jerusalem. Instead he invites them to come to Caesarea and press their charges there. What is the essence of Paul's defense before Festus and the Jewish leaders?

2. What appeal does Paul make and why? See Acts 23:11; 28:18, 19.

READ ACTS 25:13-27

3. When King Agrippa whose kingdom borders Festus' province comes with his sister Bernice to pay their respects to the new Roman governor at Caesarea, Festus uses the opportunity to discuss Paul's case. Agrippa was known as an expert in the Jewish religion.

   How does Festus put himself in the best light as he describes Paul's case to Agrippa?

   What does Festus understand about the real issue of contention between Paul and the Jewish leaders (verse 19)?

4. Why do you think Agrippa is interested in Paul's case?

   How do Paul's experiences since his arrest fulfill what the Lord predicted of Paul's future at his conversion (9:15, 16)?

5. Who is present and what is the atmosphere in the audience hall the next day (verses 23-27)?

6. What reason does Festus give for asking this audience to examine Paul's case?

7. Since Festus states his conclusion that Paul has done nothing deserving of death, why doesn't he release Paul?

READ ACTS 26:1-11

8. Why does Paul begin his defense to Agrippa as he does?

   What does Paul emphasize about his own background?

9. What does Paul insist is the reason he is on trial (verses 6-8)?

10. How would you or people you know answer Paul's question in verse 8?

11. Why does Paul describe in detail his own former actions against Jesus of Nazareth and his followers?

READ ACTS 26:12-23

12. As Paul tells King Agrippa his experience on the road to Damascus, what does he emphasize this time?

Note: Paul gives the details in verses 11, 13, 14, 17, 18 for the first time.

13. Even as he speaks, how is Paul fulfilling what God appointed him to do?

14. What would it mean for a person to change in the ways described in verse 18?

15. How have Paul's actions and message proved his obedience to Jesus' commission to him?

   How has God proved his faithfulness to Paul?

16. How does Paul relate his message to the Old Testament (verses 22, 23)?

READ ACTS 26:24-32

17. How does Festus react and why?

   How does Agrippa who professes the Jewish religion respond?

   How and why do people today act in the same ways as Festus and Agrippa when they hear the gospel message?

SUMMARY

1. The challenge and invitation of the gospel of Jesus Christ was presented to Paul, to Felix, to Festus, and to Agrippa. What did each gain and what did each lose by his decision about the gospel?

2. What do people making this decision today gain or lose?

PRAYER

Thank you, Lord, that Paul carried out your commission to bring the good news of Christ to Jews and to Gentiles, to open their eyes and turn them from darkness to light and from the power of Satan to God. Thank you that we also may receive forgiveness of our sins and a place in your kingdom. Help us to bear witness to you as faithfully as Paul did. Deliver us from fear of any modern Festus or Agrippa. For your name's sake, Amen.

DISCUSSION 12

Journey to Rome

ACTS 27 —28

Festus and Agrippa's decision that Paul deserves neither death nor imprisonment comes too late to change anything. Paul has already appealed to Caesar and this appeal once made cannot be rescinded. Luke probably was not far from Paul during his two years custody in Caesarea, and the *we* in 27:1 to 28:16 indicates his presence with Paul on the journey to Rome.

READ ACTS 27:1-20

1. Who is on the passenger list on this voyage?

   Trace the journey on your map beginning at Caesarea.

2. What do you learn about Julius, his responsibilities, and his attitude toward Paul?

3. Why is Paul's advice at Fair Havens ignored?

4. If you were writing the music score for a film about Paul's voyage, how would you express:

-the severity of this storm?

-the actions of the crew?

-their morale?

READ ACTS 27:21-38

5. When all hope is gone, what initiative does Paul take?

   What specific promise from God enables Paul to encourage his shipmates?

6. When and why do the sailors try to desert?

   What prevents their desertion?

Note: If the sailors were to leave the ship, there would not be enough skilled men to work the ship.

7. What effect do Paul's words, actions, and faith have on the sailors and others?

8. As the sailors try to run the ship up onto the beach, it hits a sandbar and the force of the waves begins to break the ship apart. How does this bear out what Paul has said before they left Fair Havens (27:9, 10)?

9. The Roman soldiers would forfeit their lives if any prisoners were to escape. Why does Julius reject their plan to kill the prisoners?

   How is Paul's faith rewarded?

10. In emergencies and danger, human beings reveal themselves for what they really are, and they show what they truly believe in. Compare Paul's actions and attitudes in this whole episode with those of the sailors and soldiers.

    What is faith in God able to do in this chapter when human skill and energy fail?

READ ACTS 28:1-10

11. What do you learn about Paul and about the natives of Melita (Malta) from the incident with the snake?

12. What effect does Paul's presence have upon the whole community?

What benefits do Paul's traveling companions gain?

What effect does the presence of Christians have upon your community?

READ ACTS 28:11-16

13. Paul has planned for a long time to go to Rome (Acts 19:21) and God confirms the rightness of his plan (Acts 23:11 and 27:23, 24). Now after many trials, Paul approaches Rome. What feelings must he have as he arrives?

What kind of welcome does Paul receive and what does it mean to him?

Note: The forum of Appius was forty-three miles from Rome, and the Three Taverns was thirty-three miles from Rome.

14. How can you explain the attitude of these Roman Christians who have never seen Paul? Remember Paul is a prisoner in chains.

READ ACTS 28:17-31

15. Three days after his arrival Paul calls together the local Jewish leaders to explain his situation to them.

What is the core of Paul's message to those who come to hear about *this sect*?

16. From the concluding verses of Acts, what do you learn about the next two years of Paul's ministry?

SUMMARY

1. After many trials and great dangers Paul has finally reached Rome, the capital of the empire. How are the reactions of those who considered Paul's message then still the choices people make today?

2. What great struggle in the book of Acts culminates in verse 28?

   How does the quotation from Isaiah explain this decision?

3. Men and women through the centuries since Paul's time have continued to proclaim the gospel that he preached. The story of Acts is not finished. What part is God asking you to play in this continuing drama?

PRAYER

Thank you, Lord Jesus, that we can expect the Holy Spirit to give us power to bear witness to you in our hometown and to the ends of the earth, even as you empowered your disciples in the first century. We are grateful that the gospel came to us because of their faithful witness. We rejoice in you, our risen living Savior, and in the privilege of serving you in our generation. Amen.

CONCLUSION

When the Lord Jesus Christ returned to the Father, he entrusted the good news about himself to a few dozen men and women who had been his disciples during his earthly ministry. All the events of the book of Acts occurred within the lifetime of that generation. What made their message, methods, and strategy so effective?

What message turned their world upside down? Jesus of Nazareth is the Son of God, the Messiah foretold in the Old Testament, proven so by his resurrection from the dead. Only through Jesus can men and women obtain forgiveness of sins. Peace with God comes by faith, not by working for it. God invites all people, Jews and Gentiles, into his family.

What methods proved so effective? In the temple and on the streets of Jerusalem, the apostles and ordinary believers became witnesses for Jesus. Those who were persecuted preached as they scattered for safety in Judea and Samaria and even to Syria.

As God broke down centuries-old barriers of race and culture, Jewish Christians began to preach to Samaritans and then to Gentiles. Paul and his companions preached in Jewish synagogues, in hired halls and market places to the Gentiles, in courtroom and prison to prosecutors, judges and guards. By such dedication and perseverance men and women from all strata of society heard the transforming message of the gospel.

What strategy launched this despised group into the beginnings of a world religion within thirty years? Paul and his companions concentrated on the leading cities of their day as the key to the evangelization of a whole region: *Antioch* in Syria, third greatest city in the Roman world; *Corinth*, trade center of the Grecian peninsula; *Ephesus*, chief city of Asia Minor; and *Rome*, capital of the Empire. The journeys included return visits to strengthen churches formed on early trips and expansion into new areas.

If persecution drove the Christian missionaries out of one town or territory, they went on to another. If arrested, they preached in jail, rejoicing that God considered them worthy of suffering for his sake.

What are the implications of this study of Acts for us? The message is still the same - **Salvation is found in no one else...no other name** (Acts 4:12).

The commission Christ gave them is ours as well - **you will receive power when the Holy Spirit comes on you; and you will be my witnesses...to the ends of the earth** (Acts 1:8).

Surely our generation needs the Good News as desperately as Paul's did. Having studied the book of Acts, let us begin to live it!

WHAT SHOULD OUR GROUP STUDY NEXT?

We recommend the Gospel of Mark, the fast paced narrative of Jesus' life, as the first book for people new to Bible study. Follow this with the Book of Acts to see what happens to the people introduced in Mark. Then in Genesis discover the beginnings of the world and find the answers to the big questions of where we came from and why we are here.

Our repertoire of guides allows great flexibility. For groups starting with *Lenten Studies*, *They Met Jesus* is a good sequel.

LEVEL 101: little or no previous Bible study experience
Mark *(recommended first unit of study)* or The Book of Mark *(Simplified English)*

Acts, Books 1 and 2
Genesis, Books 1 and 2
Psalms/Proverbs
Topical Studies
Conversations With Jesus
Lenten Studies
Foundations for Faith
Character Studies
They Met Jesus

> **Sequence for groups reaching people from non-Christian cultures**
> Foundations for Faith
> Genesis, Books 1 and 2
> Mark, Discover Jesus *or* The Book of Mark *(Simplified English)*

LEVEL 201: some experience in Bible study (after 3-4 Level 101 books)

John, Books 1 and 2
Romans
I John/James
1 Corinthians
2 Corinthians
Philippians
Colossians
Topical Studies
Prayer

Treasures
Relationships
Servants of the Lord
Change
Work – God's Gift
Celebrate
Character Studies
Four Men of God
Lifestyles of Faith, Books 1 and 2

LEVEL 301: More experienced in Bible study

Matthew, Books 1 and 2
Galatians & Philemon
1 and 2 Peter
Hebrews
1 and 2 Thessalonians, 2 & 3 John
Isaiah
Ephesians

Topical Studies
Set Free
Character Studies
David
Moses
Biweekly or Monthly Groups *may use topical studies or character studies.*

ABOUT NEIGHBORHOOD BIBLE STUDIES

Neighborhood Bible Studies, Inc. is a leader in the field of small group Bible studies. Since 1960, NBS has pioneered the development of Bible study groups that encourage each member to participate in the leadership of the discussion.

The mission of Neighborhood Bible Studies is to: Mobilize and empower followers of Jesus Christ to introduce and multiply small group discussion Bible studies among their neighbors, co-workers, and friends so that participants can encounter God, grow in faith, and pattern their lives after Jesus.

The vision of Neighborhood Bible Studies is to: Invite people everywhere to a relationship with Christ through the study of God's word.

Publication in more than 20 languages indicates the versatility of NBS cross culturally. NBS **methods and materials** are used around the world to:

Equip individuals for facilitating discovery Bible studies
Serve as a resource to the church

Skilled NBS personnel provide consultation by telephone or e-mail. In some areas, they conduct workshops and seminars to train individuals, clergy, and laity in how to establish small group Bible studies in neighborhoods, churches, workplaces and specialized facilities. **Call 1-800-369-0307 to inquire about consultation or training.**

ABOUT THE FOUNDERS

Marilyn Kunz and Catherine Schell, authors of many of the NBS guides, founded Neighborhood Bible Studies and directed its work for thirty-one years. Currently other authors contribute to the series.

ABOUT THE AUTHORS

Virginia Bowen and Lorraine Fleischman spent over 35 years in Japan as missionaries. Together with a number of Japanese Christians they founded Seisho o Yomu Kai (SYK), the Japanese expression of Neighborhood Bible Studies, and directed its work until their retirement in 1987. SYK continues under Japanese direction. The Japanese edition of *Foundations for Faith* is available from the Dobbs Ferry Office.

The cost of your study guide has been subsidized by faithful people who give generously to NBS. For more information, visit our web site: www.neighborhoodbiblestudy.org   *1-800-369-0307*

Complete Listing of NBS Study Guides

Getting Started
How to Start a Neighborhood Bible Study *(handbook & video or audio cassette)*

Bible Book Studies
Genesis, Book 1 *Begin with God*
Genesis, Book 2 *Discover Your Roots*
Psalms & Proverbs *Journals of Wisdom*
Isaiah *God's Help Is on the Way*
Matthew, Book 1 *God's Promise Kept*
Matthew, Book 2 *God's Purpose Fulfilled*
Mark *Discover Jesus*
Luke *Good News and Great Joy*
John, Book 1 *Explore Faith and Understand Life*
John, Book 2 *Believe and Live*
Acts, Book 1 *The Holy Spirit Transforms Lives*
Acts, Book 2 *Amazing Journeys with God*
Romans *A Reasoned Faith*
1 Corinthians *Finding Answers to Life's Questions*
2 Corinthians *The Power of Weakness*
Galatians & Philemon *Fully Accepted by God*
Ephesians *Living in God's Family*
Philippians *A Message of Encouragement*
Colossians *Staying Focused on Truth*
1 & 2 Thessalonians, 2 & 3 John, Jude *The Coming of the LORD*
Hebrews *Access to God*
1 & 2 Peter *Strength Amidst Stress*
1 John & James *Faith that Lives*

Topical Studies
Celebrate *Reasons for Hurrahs*
Conversations with Jesus *Getting to Know Him*
Change *Facing the Unexpected*
Foundations for Faith *The Basics for Knowing God*
Lenten Studies *Life Defeats Death*
Prayer *Communicating with God*
Relationships *Connect to Others: God's Plan*
Servants of the LORD *Embrace God's Agenda*
Set Free *Leaving Negative Emotions Behind*
Treasures *Discover God's Riches*
Work - God's Gift *Life-Changing Choices*

Character Studies
Four Men of God *Unlikely Leaders*
Lifestyles of Faith, Book One *Choosing to Trust God*
Lifestyles of Faith, Book Two *Choosing to Obey God*
They Met Jesus *Life-Changing Encounters*
David *Passions Pursued*
Moses *Learning to Lead*

Simplified English
The Book of Mark *The Story of Jesus*